Write Me Back To Book

Chioma Ikpa

Presentation by *BookLeaf Publishing*

Web: www.bookleafpub.com

E-mail: info@bookleafpub.com

ISBN: 9789357612784

First edition 2022

DEDICATION

This book is dedicated to Jehovah Shammah,
my ever-present help.

ACKNOWLEDGEMENT

First and foremost, thank you God for pulling
me through, thank you for the good and the bad
because without it I wouldn't be who I am or
where I am. This book wrote itself because you
held the pen. A thousand tongues would never
be enough to capture who you are to me but
thank you for being my rock.

I would like to thank the lovely team at Book
Leaf Publishing for presenting this opportunity. I
have had a growing desire to publish a set of
poems for a while now so thank you for creating
a process that is so seamless.

Thank you to my friends and family for
supporting my poetry journey so far, for every
piece you shared, for every word of
encouragement you've given me, for investing in
my creativity, and for your strength. It keeps me
going.

Thank you to Modupe, for recommending this
challenge.

PREFACE

I grew up an observant child, a deep thinker; very quiet with a very loud mind. I have always loved reading Dr Seuss books and loved how lighthearted and illustrative they were. I feel deeply and like many of you, I have known emotional turmoil, deep ridden anxiety, hurt, betrayal, pain to break or build you. I have also known love, a lot of it. As this perfectly imperfect soul wandered through life, I found that opportunities to use poetry kept arising and every time I picked up the pen there was almost this rush of creativity just waiting to be released. Writing became an adventure for me and gradually I started to hone my craft as a Creative Storyteller, sharing my heart at faith-based events at university, as part of election campaigns and to help inspire and provoke thought, generally. I have now set up a social platform called Word Your Word, Where Creativity Meets Truth. The heartland for this platform is women but my hope is to also shed light on how words can change the world around us and perception. Sometimes our thoughts tell us stories that aren't true and I believe words can shape-shift reality.

Fast-forward to 25 year old me, I have decided to take on this challenge because I believe poetry can be a tool for change, although not often regarded as highly, beyond anthology.

There Is No Me Without You

This is the other world
Where water makes its collision course
Where waves paint white rocks brown
And the sun coats the surface silver
One of our natural treasures
A canopy covering the oceans deep
A blanket, an emblem of peace
An expanse of promise
It's depth and breadth a wonder
Wonder parades this mind of mine
As my feet collide with the tide
It WAS tide, sun, and sand
Till it was water and waste
And the shore an open door to debris
Wonder if the world underwater still breaths
Still beats
If tranquility still speaks for the derelict
In the oceans deep
A spectacle you are
To fill any space you occupy
A rarity you are
To give and take my breath away
A danger we must be to use and abuse the mouth
that feeds
The arms that hold firm the ships at seas

There's no me without you
So I pledge to treat you honourably

Freedom Has A Sound

What an imperfect paradise you find yourself in
A two faced dream promising forever yet ending
so soon
What a paradoxical world it seems
The outstretched hands you once knew drew
intimacy, now bite at your palms angry -
treachery is
Hidden in the crevice of your subconscious
You never saw clearly
Who knew dependency would cost
Now with a hardened heart, hands clasped
Your reflection is broken glass
When all you ever wanted was to be loved
All you ever wanted was to be seen
All you ever needed was a piece of hope
You hoped would light the fire in your bones
Bones may hold me up but I felt like words
brought me down
Beat me sullen, shy, sunken
Buttoned the speaker in me draped in silence
Till childhood dreams became luxuries you only
visit at the movies
Rejection will teach you to love - with an iron
fist, feelings masked

To wait for permission to do something
different, outside the box
To crave affection from anyone who shows you
attention
And self-destruct whenever your worth is
questioned
I'm an avid believer that freedom has a sound
If you only you choose to let it out
If you accepted the past and gave present you a
chance
Chance it.
I promise of you miss the moon you'll still see
the stars
I can assure you that words don't hurt as much as
an unfulfilled heart
I know that you've had a rough start
I know that life keeps laughing in darts
You're not target practise so shake it off
And know that you're loved
Know that you're essential, important resilient,
special
There's noone on this planet that is like you
Release your sound of freedom
And do you
It's time to let go

Selfish Ambition

Candid conversations
On the contrary hidden motivations
That's the middle man
We all know it
Own it
It's a dog eat dog world
So grab a lion
Climb the chain
Stop.
Do you have enough to sustain that jump
Far above your ceiling made of stone
Chiselled into frame
Over years of self defamation
There has to be room for you to roam free
Own your identity
Bank on it
It may just be your ticket
To living your best life

In The Thick Of Life

Last chance
To give this heart respite
To give this breath life

Just a starry night or a moment on a scorching
summers day
To purge the pain away

Just a little extension with whatever's trending
That will do it

Just a picture
Maybe the attention will cure it

Just a touch, anything to feel anything but this
Maybe the screams will drown these sorrows
Maybe the night will numb tomorrow

Just a day off duty
Where dogs don't eat dogs
Where peace meets the serene
And moments of starless sombre dwindle and
wander into obscurity

Just a day where expectation echoes true

Where words don't war me boundless
Where my weakness is not dangled like a prized
jewel
And weighted against the selfish

Just a moment
Where my purse is no longer a leaking tap
Where my phone functions for me
and not to mould me

Into boxes

Carbon copies

These things may well come home
But I don't know if they'll ever be firm enough to
build upon
Strong enough to withstand the fire
Soft enough to wade in forever
Peace enough for me to exhale
Deep enough for me to get lost in anything
but this...
This little heart beats and battles bricks
But battles build resilience
In the thick of life

Culture

A coat of credence
Drilled into your genesis
A language
Channelled by the young and old
An heirloom worn with honour
Home.
Engrained through every sound
Every smell a memory made
Every place we congregate
A movie in motion
A celebration
Of culture

Come Alive

If eyes could speak, it would tell me where the spec is
If mouths could hear, it would be sparing with words
If hands could think, it would hold onto love
If ears could discern we would be wiser
If a nose could sing, it would be an ectasy of melody and anguish
Song and sorrow
Forever more

The High School Experience

Popularity is a nerds prize and
Praise for the lonely child
And beggars are choosers when there's no light
in their eyes.
Relationships are imperative
Love is optional
It's a pyramid but there's no climbing at all
Know your place
Know your seat
You aren't smart
You're weak
You're weird
You're rude
You're fat
You're cute
In a room full of opinions can you hear your
own voice
Can you feel the clasp of lies chipping away at
you
Chasing you down
In the short but lengthy paradigm
of high school

Little Quaint House

Wrapped in this little quaint house
Memories arise till it's expendable and we make
new ones memorable
The mind is a portal to paradise
Like you're living in two places at the same time
Your home
Your mind
Shoes intertwine and huddle like a shiver
Doors creak and ceilings steep
Floors grazed, chairs cave
It's a quaint hideout but there's no hiding here
It's a training ground where only the daring dare
to bear the pitta patta of tiny feet
The scuffles of rodents burrowing holes in the
concrete
You must be hospitable by force
They've made it clear they're not going
anywhere else

In this little quaint home you learn patience
You find ingenuity in the weirdest spaces
You run many races
All to the same places
Same teacher

Different lessons
In this little quaint home of mine

A Mind On A Mission

The young mind travels
In contention for what awaits it
The future is always present
In every still moment
It finds it way
Hoping for what cannot be seen, eagerly waiting
yet frustrated with uncertainty
It reckons with its idols that emulate the end
goal
While time weaps at the time it let go
Hoping tomorrow might actually come into its
own
And breath again.
Live again.
Be present once more.
Today needs you
Come back home

Part Of A Portrait

I can't choose my reflection
I am a reflection of everything
Genetics, upbringing
Every scar a tale of travail
Every smile a glimmer of hope

I am a product of love
Though not sustained
I am the hope that love happens and can happen
again

I am bold
I am the candle but I'm also the match stick
Fragile but powerful
I am light
Made to shine bright

I can't choose my reflection
I am a reflection of everything
Words, Actions, Atmosphere, Grace
Nature, Nurture, Favour, Faith
I am made in his image

Remember

You WERE small, now stand tall
Like a sponge absorb it all
Like a lego tower build
Like a door SHIELD yourself from the wind
Don't get caught up in it
It's a big big ocean
It's a big big world
You've become the lion after the snail
You grew but honey couldn't you tell
At the bottom of that deep dark well
I hope you know life is a gift
I hope you treasure everyday you're blessed with
And like fins amidst the waves
Courage will carry you for the rest of your days

Candlelight

Like a light light the way
Shine bright
The night calls you to take a stand
Mount yourself up
Stand as light
Like a beacon beckoning to be seen
You dream and dream and dream
But a little flicker never hurt anyone
A little glimmer makes the eyes grow fonder
I wonder when darkness took the reigns
To campaign for first place
Must've been when we traded candles for
lampshades
Candlelight
Shine bright

Rainbow's and Reality

There is a joy that pours from the core
Sealed in promise
Watered in waiting
There is a place worth saving
A mind worth knowing
A hand worth holding
A dream unfolding

Even in the silence
There is a sound of hope
Even in the noise
There is a heart that beats for life
That lives for thrills and chills
The extraordinary things
Something's change when we make us a priority
When we actualise thoughts
Step by step
Day by Day
Every dream a rainbow
In the realm of reality

Faith

Walking on water
Trusting the father
A consolation felt
A redemptive shield

A nonchalant wind
A smile and a sigh
The creak of sunrise
A plane in the sky

Patience and perseverance
Lessons and lectures
It's a seed sown
Where promise roams

When it all goes down
It will come back up
It's a gift of love
From a timeless God

Architect Of The Earth

Listen, she calls out
High above the hilltops
Hear, understanding raises her voice
Summons a crowd
Deception may bear witness but it doesn't rank
where she stands
She releases a sound
And from her comes good judgement
Knowledge and discernment
More valuable than silver
More precious than gold

Formed before time began
In her hand lies
The courage of kings
On her waist
The belt of truth
At her gate
Joy to sustain

Wisdom is her name
Proverbs 8

Seal The Standard

I have an assignment
Before you walk through that door
Remember who you came in with
Write it down
Treasure it
It doesn't shift if people don't fit
It isn't open
To negotiation

If you were a farmer would you sell your land
If you were a tree would you sell your seed
If you were a king would you trade your crown
The answer is no
Every time

No I will not morph into your paradox of
misshapen truths
No I will not bury my virtue because you asked
me to
No I will not shrink so you can shine
No I will not stop striving for what's mine

It's your life.
Live it like it matters
Because it does

Time: The Broken Tape Recorder

Time will always move but change doesn't come
imminently.
Our transgressions unwittingly mirrored
In the obscene, the obscure, the obsolete
We love languidly
And loathe loudly
Trade jewels for jokers
Extol puppeteers, anyone with the chest to
impress
We're in the wild wild west
Where South eats North
And escapism is a cup of coffee
Choice a child
Will we ever be adult enough

We've known time will always betray us
But change is the resistance
Transformation
Love
Even if they don't reciprocate
Even if your hand hangs for a little bit
Solidarity will rise
For as long as The Father presides
Beyond the crux of time

Growth Hurts

The uncomfortable is a fortress of fact and
fiction
A charge
A necessary one
A journey on hinge, like a tight rope
An elastic that will stretch as far as you go
It is a war-zone
You will know pain
The heart kind
And therein lies-lies
The stubborn kind
You will find your mind reckoning with the shift
Grieving the old

Growth hurts.
A lot
But we cloak our plight in the bright lights
Too sky to address it
Change is an egregious delight
In the world we inhabit

The fact is we are built to bounce back
But with that we are also created to feel
Through the growth pains
Through the mind games

Through the panic attacks

Take a moment
Pause. Breathe. Reflect.
And as we forge forward into the new
Future you will thank you
Forever and a day

9 789357 612784